I0140904

Connecting Memories – Book 2

An Adult Coloring Book Designed With 27
Simple Familiar Color Cued Drawings And Sentence Cuing Phrases
- For Cognitive Art Therapy -

Recommended As A Resource For Therapeutic Recreation Departments
And At Home One On One With A Care Taker Or Family Member

27 Single Sided Coloring Pages

———————

The Adult Coloring Book Craze is Here. And now the older
adults can join in on the fun and enjoy the benefits too.

Bonnie has created a great activities resource for elders with
dementia that can be used individually, on a one on one basis
or in a group setting. Simple familiar designs, color cuing
and common phrases allow for successful completion.
Providing a positive, calm and fun experience.

I highly recommend its use with anyone with cognitive impairment.
Every therapeutic recreation department should utilize this amazing
resource as they will immediately see the benefits to their elders.

Recommended By: Alexis Chiucarello, Director Of Therapeutic Recreation
And Dementia Program Coordinator Long Term Center

———————

Illustrator & Author: Bonnie S. MacLachlan
Publisher: Art.Z Illustrations
Griswold, Ct
www.ArtZillustrations.com
Special Thanks To: Alexis Chiucarello

Made In America

Home _____ Home

I Love _____ Cupcakes

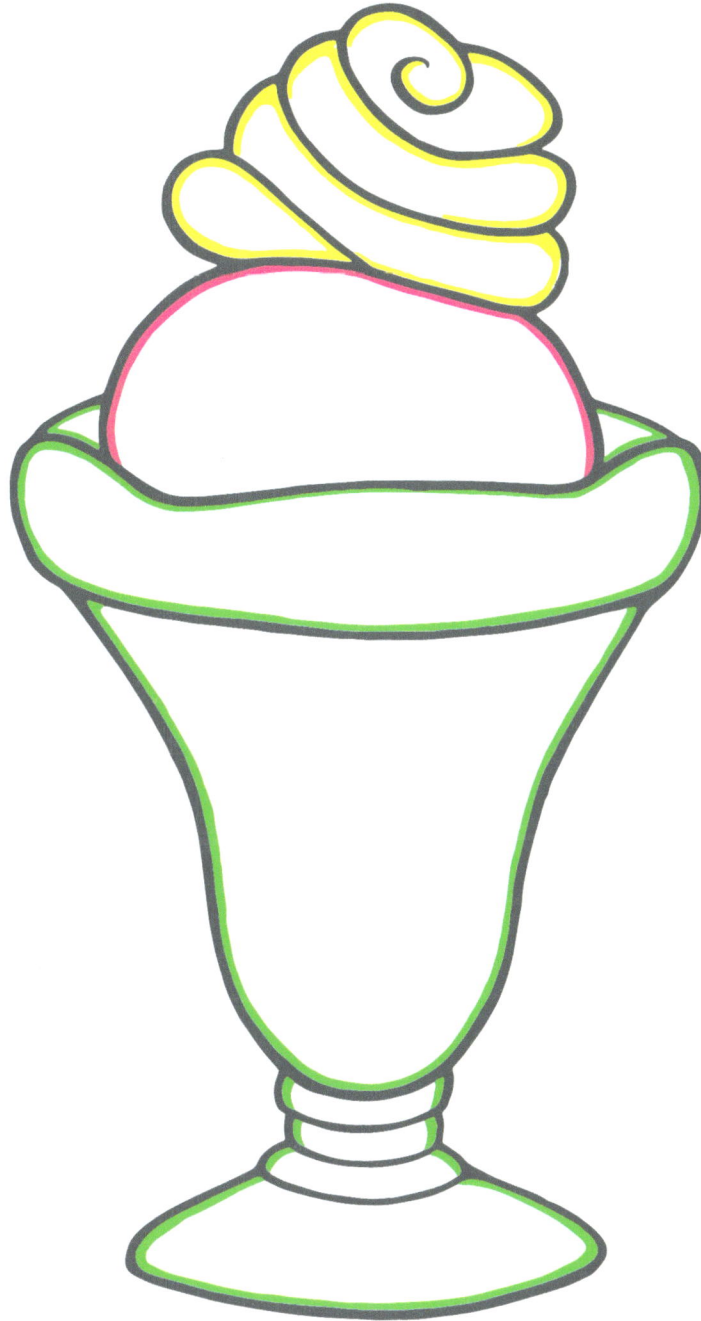

Hot Fudge _____ Are Delicious

Jelly

_____ And Jelly

Tea and _____

Pots And _____

Bluebird On My _____

A Tree Grows In _____

_____ Leaf

Watering My _____ Garden

Flowers Make Me _____

Apple Pie And _____

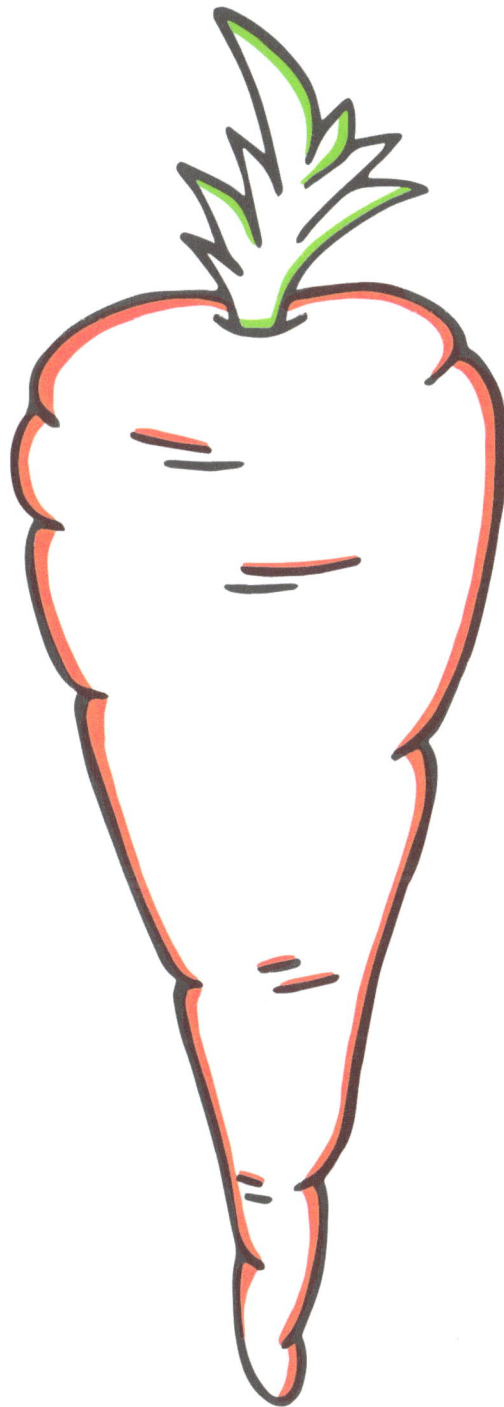

Carrots and _____

Mushroom _____

I Love My Pretty _____ Hat

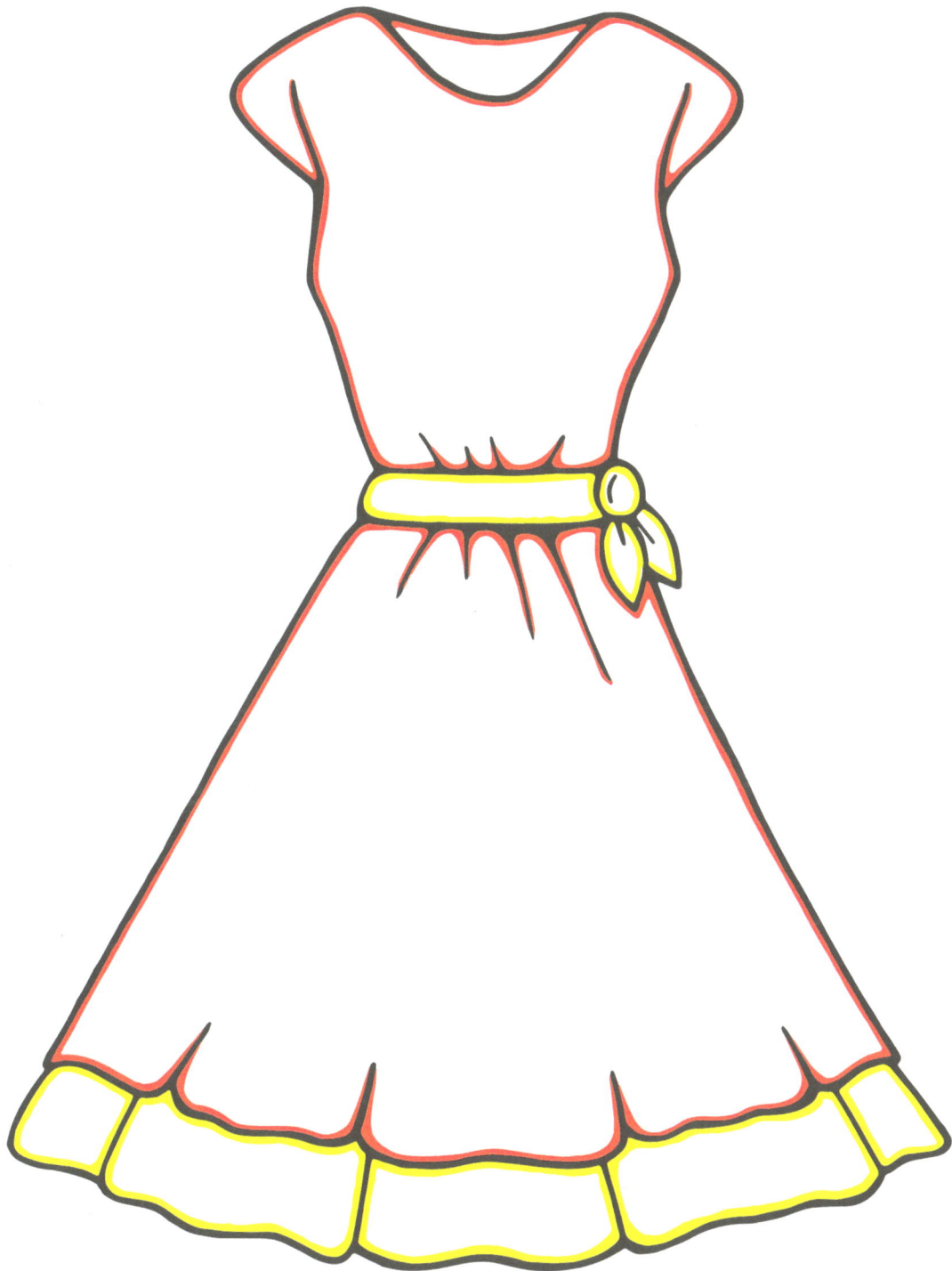

My Favorite _____ Dress

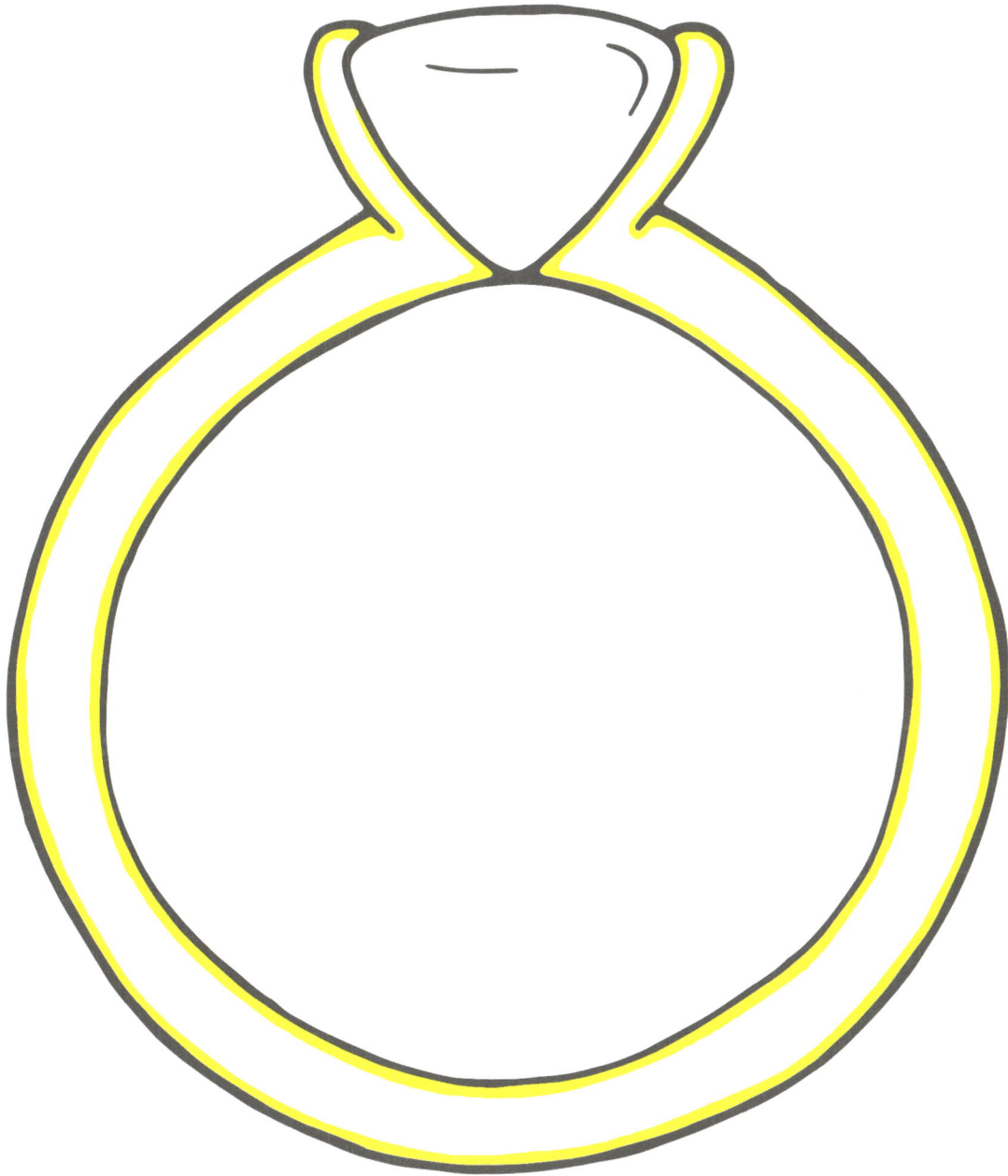

_____ Ring

I Have A _____
In My Pocketbook

_____ Shoes

I Brush My Teeth Every _____

The Shirt Off My _____

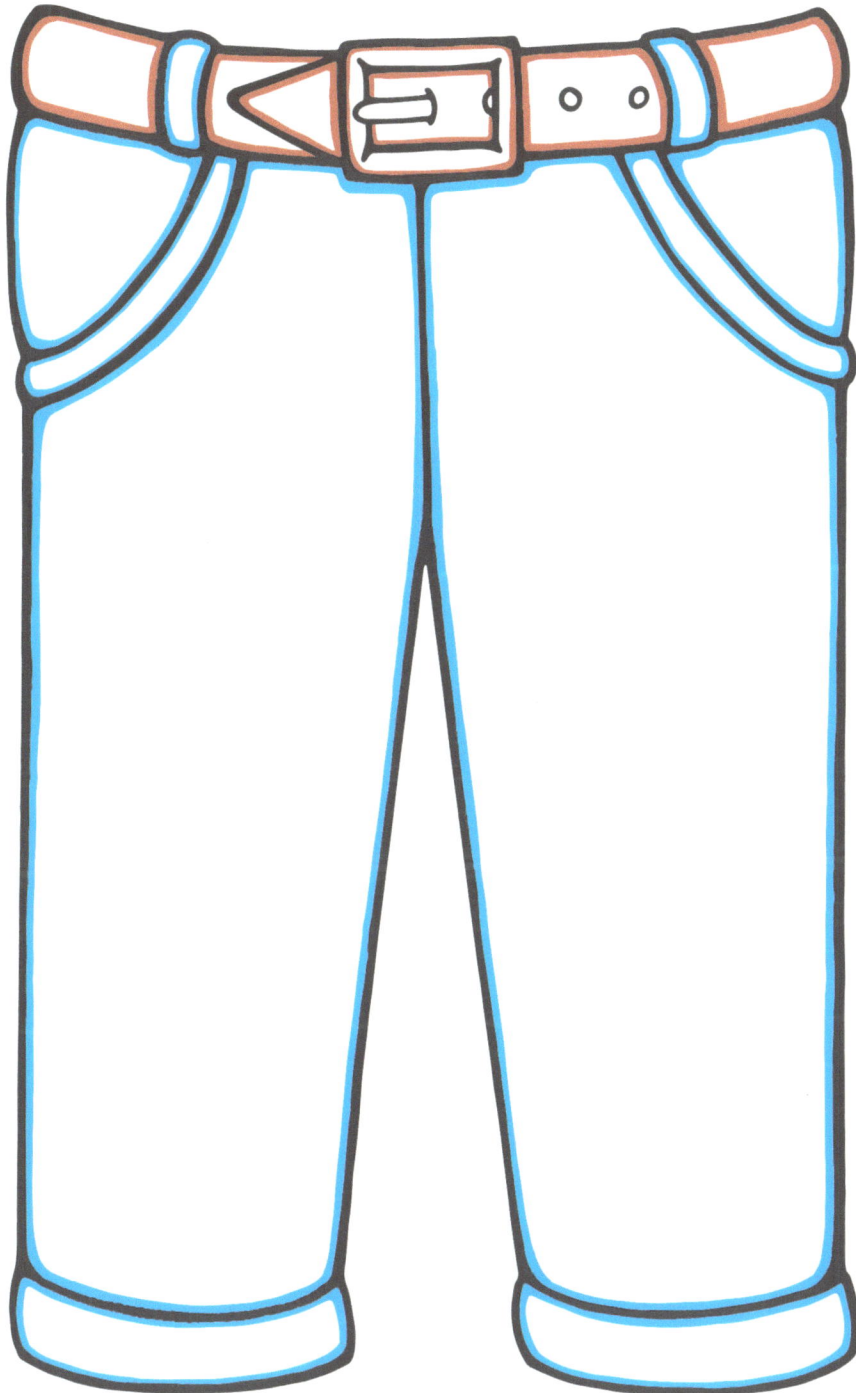

I Wear The Pants In The _____

If The Shoe _____

It's Time To Go _____

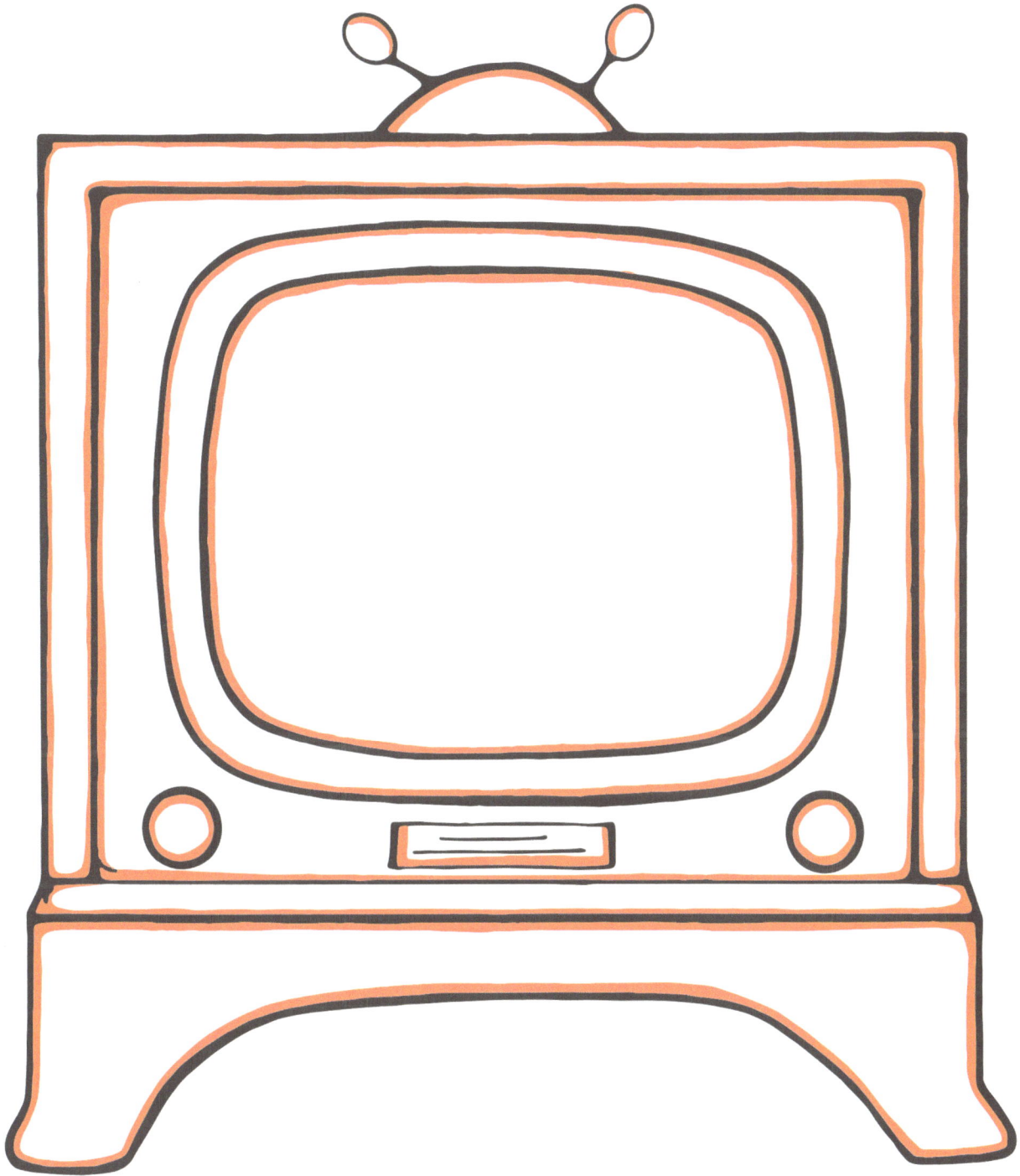

I Watch _____
On The Television

Hammer And _____

Sawing _____